Remorseless Loyalty

Poems by

Christine Gelineau

The Ashland Poetry Press
Ashland University
Ashland, Ohio 44805

The author wishes to make grateful acknowledgment of the vital support of family and friends, most especially, Stephen, Courtney and Jonathan, Gregory, Janine, Catharine Foote and Peggy Sise. Also to Maxine Kumin, Ruth Stone, Molly Peacock, Maria Mazziotti Gillan, Enid Shomer, Milton Kessler, Liz Rosenberg, Chad Davidson, Michael Czarnecki and others, whose encouragement was sustaining at the moments when I needed it.

Grateful acknowledgment is made to the editors of the following journals and anthologies in which these poems first appeared, sometimes in a slightly different form:

Green Mountains Review, "Persephone Converses with the Snow," "Carpe Diem"
Natural Bridge, "Bliss"
Connecticut Review, "Stand By," "Orison" and "Spring Again"
Runes: A Review of Poetry, "Brainstorm"
Louisiana Literature, "Modus Operandi," "The Attraction of Hurricanes," and "Christmas in St. Petersburg, 1966"
Paterson Literary Review, "The Suicide's Mother," "List for a Blue Day," "Survivor," "Naming the Child" and "Reply to Sirens"
Seneca Review, "Rite"
American Literary Review, "Dolls"
The American Voice, "Pulse"
Kalliope, "A Short Poem about the Long Poem" and "Putting the Filly Down"
The Beloit Poetry Journal, "Inheritance" and "Cast"
Mediphors, "Please Don't Wave"
Kansas Quarterly/Arkansas Review, "Endow" under the title "Sestina"
Kansas Quarterly, "Particles"
The Florida Review, "Crochet"
Movieworks, "Mirrored"
Poetry Now, "Gelding the Two-Year-Old"
Mona Poetica, "Comparing Scars"
"Pulse," "The Green Road," "Iridescent," and "Picking Peaches" appear in the chapbook, *In the Greenwood World* (Foothills Publishing)

Printed in the United States of America

ISBN: 0-912592-57-5

Library of Congress Catalog Card Number: 2005933427

Book cover design by Janine Gelineau

Calla lilly x-ray photograph © Steven Myers

Book cover background photo by Janine Gelineau

Contents

Inheritance

Remorseless Loyalty

for Stephen

Inheritance

Putting the Filly Down

Dead

small click of a word to last so long.

It's the improbably soft
and lively look
of her mane I won't forget.

The body being small, they
lashed her by the pasterns to a chain
across the empty arms of a bucket loader
and lifted her inverted in the air. The arms
held her out before the tractor like an offering,
and she rode that way to the grave
in stiff dignity, save for the mocking
animation of her mane, silken
and playful in the face of February.

No ceremony or Astroturf disguises here:
this grave is raw-lipped and greedy
as any hole you ever fill
with something you'd spent love on.

Inheritance

I
am the
woman they give
dead women's
clothes to
I live easily   grass-green
in them, my   zebras loosed
friend's mother's   in ivory
print dress with   space
or
my own
mother's
bracelet:
her opalescent
hearts clasp
my wrist   the continuing
comfort-   significance of
ably I   dead women's
can never   shoes even
outwalk   the cold
I
wrap out
with the autumn
orange wool
of an
inherit-
ed
coat   wardrobe
mine   of chance
is the   of well-
worn
inevitability
none other
suits

A Short Poem About the Long Poem

The lyric poem then is
that moment in which you realize
your daughter's horse has
stepped into downed wire
and will surely panic.

In that suspended moment, the lyric
lets you off, releases you:
burned with the memory to be sure
but freed, loosed
in the space the lyric leaves
for the silences to speak.

The longer poem by contrast
requires you to stay mounted;
to watch her face
as the mare bolts, to pound
after her as if you could
control, rather than only
uncover over time, what must
come next: the mare racing riderless
and the still form curled
where it fell, nested motionless in the grass.

There is, you know, a desire
to remain with the unresolved
moment: the mare nearly
to the horizon, stirrups akimbo
and the reins blown out,
empty. There is a
desire never to ask
the only things that matter
for fear of what the answers might be.

The long poem asks
you to dismount
and go to her.

Endow

What's it like there, Mother?
Have you been there long enough
to be happy? Have your bones
cleaned off to silver now, holy and exact?
You did so love to dress
in pure lines and simple elegance.

That insistent black elegance
was your signature here, Mother,
but it was Dad and I who chose the dress
that you wore last and we had had enough
of black. We put you in the teal, an exact
gesture; by now, soil-black and moist, your bones

wear only what becomes the bones.
Even the outerwear of mahogany elegance
we gave has softened into exactly
the embrace we had intended. Mother,
that last evening we talked, I remember well enough
the look of you in white: the white dress

the hospital issues; the room dressed
white, white ceiling, white walls, bone-
white bedclothes, your face floating in whiteness enough
to release you; your hand in white air, elegantly
waving goodbye, goodbye; so like you, Mother,
to be, even at that moment, exact.

But it was more than I could imagine you would exact
of me the black sophistication of a funeral dress
while you wore blue and wouldn't leave your box, Mother.
Sucked down with grief to a model's high cheek-boned
look, I came into a sudden, adolescent elegance
but paid for it. Can we ever pay enough?

Even decades have not been time enough
to compensate the cost. The exacting
interweave of you and me, that elegant
embroidery of dreams, demands, losses and redress,
continues to work its intricate details, the bone
needles pulling bright venous threads, Mother.

I wear our crewelwork close to the skin and dress
to camouflage the truth: we each are silver at the bone,
and what you must endow, I must inherit, Mother.

Modus Operandi

I am a fisher
    my rig deep
in secret water

My lures are tinsel
  bright;   they grin with hooks
     silver aqua coquettes
they wink to the fish
     their feather fins awriggle.

I like my fish cooked
  whole
       the eye unflinching
the tail crisp   brittle from the fire

and the slender bones
     concealed in flesh
like smooth smiles.

Open Range

There's a wilderness
in every child: horses
manifested mine, galloping
through a West I knew only
from books and Saturday morning
TV, a vista of chaparral
and sky into which my literary
horses continually escaped,
their great hearts twisting in their chests
as they soared out of the stockade.

I taught myself to canter
on two legs, to snort
and nicker and fought my mother
to grow my mane out,
a seine for the wind.

That luminous river of their bodies,
the pulse of those staccato hooves remains
a scouring wind within me still:
the far off horizon line of hills
undulates as we run, waving
its welcome, waving
its limitless farewells.

Del's Lemonade

It's awkward to talk about it.
I was six... maybe seven...
headed to the library...
This was the fifties in suburban Cranston, Rhode Island
and even careful mothers like my own
let their six year olds go off alone
on a twenty minute hike to the library,
a trust she never had occasion to regret.

It was summer, hot, and I remember I wore
the little black-and-white skirt
with matching panties sewn right in like a skater's skirt.
I had a white halter top to go with it, wide eyelet ruffle
all around the neckline and my chaste middle,
cool and smooth, between the cropped top and the little skirt.
My mother brushed my hair into a high pony tail
above each ear, then knotted a ribbon at the tip of the tail
and twirled the hair into sleek rolls finished off with a bow.
It's how Princess Leia probably wore her hair as a child.

We lived at the bottom of Rose Hill Drive, last house on the road.
There was an undeveloped field beside us
and a Del's Frozen Lemonade stand
next to the house across the street.
Bruce DeLuca's father owned all the Del's—
making the people who worked there
in my mind, not exactly "strangers"—
so when the man behind the counter called to me
as I crossed their lot carrying my little stack
of library returns, I was shy but not alarmed.

"Little girl, do you want a lemonade?" he asked.
I was confused and a little embarrassed;
"I don't have any money," I stammered.
"That's okay," he said, handing down the lemonade,

condensation already beading the cup
and suddenly I understood the exchange exactly:

it stirred something in adults just to look at me,
I was that pretty as a child. The lemonade

went down chill and sweet
as any unearned privilege.

Reply to Sirens

Urgent ambulance,
aflare with lights,
passes on the highway

and it is Diane
I think of. Really, the
only clear memory I have
of that cousin, and it's
coupled to ambulances' wails
as inextricably as Pavlov's
dogs are linked to bells:

sirens keen and Diane
and I are children, side-by-side
in bed in our Mémère's
upstairs room, knowing
neither one another nor
the room very well, and so
huddling back to back into
the solace of one another's
humanness in the unmoored openness
of unfamiliar shadows and half-light.

A siren sounded out there
in the city neither of us lived in
and Diane whispered, "Sister
Mary Francis told us to say
three Hail Marys when you
hear a siren, to help the people"
so we hunkered, and we prayed
"Holy Mary, Mother of God,
pray for us now..."

Like a chain letter you
dare not break, I'm
praying still.

The evening that the sirens
screamed for me, I never
even heard them. I remember
trying to pinpoint where
I was hurt: "Watch that arm!"
I heard when they lifted me;
I had no clue. Pain was too
encompassing to get it to focus
in one place more than in another.
I was pain, and pain was me;
exactly the sort of simple
integration of self which in
the abstract we can persuade
ourselves we would admire.

Though I never heard that siren I
remember listening with aloof
curiosity to the voices inside the ambulance:
my own, praying the Our Father like
a mantra to distance the pain; the attendants
grumbling to me to be quiet, and most
of all Karl's voice praying: "I can't
breathe I can't breathe I can't..."

Decades pass and the sirens
echo in me as they always have:
Hail Mary or Our Father—
superstitious
as my maiden Irish aunt
and as wholly
unwilling to give up
the long comfort
of human voices
raised together in the dark.

Crochet

My mother
my self
my daughter

yarn hooked
through itself
in chain stitch

woven from
one another
into one another

nurtured,
or contained?
the chained strand

stronger than
yarn alone
and treacherously soft.

Orison

Lilacs, like a plush-robed choir
at their daily office, the perfume
of their voices lofts the Gregorian air,
a sisterhood at chant: ripe,
womanly, decorous, the reiterating
harmonies of their flowerets an incense,
rococo musk into which
swim the bees
      the bacchanalian
   bees
     alleluia

New

You're nine walking
to school in April air so new
your chest aches:

the maples unwrap translucent
ears, tuning them towards you;
tulips in the yards spread

their petal lips in expectant smiles
as you pass while redwings
whistle the high note

of your heart; the sun streams directly
into your dreams, your every prayer

prepares itself to be answered

Letter to My Rapist

Wrapped in summer's green-black dark
we slept, lulled to dreaming in
the insect hum, while you unzipped
the dining room window's screen
with the small, precisely sharp
knife you later held to my throat.

Did you see the ground floor bedroom
where the baby slept, curled in that
high-backed hump, little pulse of flesh,
heart in a box of bars? Was it
the hatch of crib bars in the night
light's glow that kept you clear of her?

Why didn't even the dogs awaken
in their crates? confined, contented
in their molded plastic dens, while
you mounted stair by stair to where
I slept on the side of the bed
Stephen would use if he'd been home.

The first flash of knowing may have been
the worst, your hands already on me
in a sudden end to dreams. Was that
the instant that satisfied you most?

How orderly it was.
How well we understood
the way things would unfold.

You burnt off my sense of touch,
of smell, of self with the hot metal
of your hands, the acrid smelt
of your sweat and sperm, the mutilation
of your knife where only lovers
and infants had come before.

This need not have happened
to have happened: you wait for me,
for any woman, there
in every darkness.

Dolls

The mothers seem already
to have forgotten.

Dolls emerge from tissue
and the mothers admire
the honey-thick hair, lash-lined
china eyes, the crisp dresses.

What the mothers have forgotten
children know unfailingly.

Children croon
to the frozen faces, their own
faces reflect inverted
in the aggie eyes.

Vinyl shoes and small dresses
are left to closets or the underworld
of beds. Dynel hair
knots and features grime while
the children and the blank-trunked
dolls rehearse their
lock-kneed goosestep.

Dolls serenely ride
the dump trucks, aeroplanes,
or roller skates straight
into tragic accidents.

Pale eyes roll shut
in their heads as they fall.

No matter.

In the night those eyes
click open wide. Smiling

their paralyzed smiles
dolls leave the shelves, the beds.

Deep in the darkness
each knows exactly
how to find us.

Rocky Point: First Love

Seen from the Rocky Point Ferris wheel at night,
Narragansett Bay has a tromp de oeil serenity.
I was just fourteen, dizzy with the height
and with being there with Dan. The far
bay's look of calm helped to steady the woozy
feel it gave me to be aloft in air, casually
suspended high above the dirty pavement.

The memory I hold is slow motion and exact:
cradled together in the narrow car, his arm sweetly
settled on my shoulder as we rise by stages
from the others we have come with. We wheel
steadily to the zenith and rock there together
in the sea-salt, light-jeweled summer dark,
and never does the wheel descend.

Picking Peaches

Even before we're close enough
to reach to them we smell
the sweet offertory of their ripening.

Birds lift with loud reluctance
leaving behind opened suns
of soft-fleshed fruit.

He steadies the ladder
while I rise among the leaves
handing down the warm-skinned globes.

Peach by peach they drop
from my fingers to the cradle
of his outstretched hands

and for that moment we
too are as filled to the skin
as fruit.

Christmas in St. Petersburg, 1966

I didn't even know any photographs survived of that trip
but here's one of those oddly-shaped snaps
Mémère's Brownie box camera used to take:
the five of us lined up awkwardly, not quite
touching, individually squinting
into the Florida sun.

What strikes me is the sheer bulk
of the four near-grown children.
Centered among us, our father looks
diminished, a forty-seven year old man
who has brought his children home
to his mother's house for Christmas.

His tender smallness under the stark
blue of that southern sky recalls to me
four months before the photograph was taken:

the five of us waiting
in the church vestibule behind
the sleek mahogany of my mother's coffin,
so small, so tender
even a sixteen year old had sense enough
to step up and take his hand
for the long walk down the aisle.

Naming the Child

If poetry is language charged
with meaning then we'll
never write a tighter poem
than this: to name the child.

Before I was born, my parents had
picked out *Maureen* for the "girl name."
I arrived as we all did then
into a blaze of strangers, my
mother anesthetized, removed.
By the time she saw me first,
the nurses had me tidied up, wrapped
and dried; they laid me swaddled
in her arms. *Christine Marie*, my
mother thought at once, as if
I'd come already named. *Christine Marie*,
my given name in some pure sense,
some echo my parents caught
of religion's reach to meanings:
re-ligare, a name which ties me
as ligament binds the bone,
back to sources,
genesis and family.

When my own children were born, I
wished for that givenness, that sure
voice in the cosmic soup. But I wished
in the silence and we named as best we could,
anxious to choose a word, condensed as
anthracite, as diamond, a ligament
of language, not alone to bind
the child to us, but sinew as well
to strengthen
for the journeying away.

for Courtney and Gregory

Please Don't Wave

The highway's busy enough that
even the sixth grader understands
my coming to their bus stop with them:
but it goes no farther. "Watch
us cross from here, Mom, and,"
pleads the second grader,
"please don't wave."

His sister's kisses—given when we
sight the bus a quarter mile down
the valley—stay on my lips in waxy
passionfruit lipsmacker. They're almost
the age we were that upside down
August you waved to me, Mother.
Please don't wave.

The family took two cars down to the Cape:
our adolescent initiation. You and Dad
left early for the wedding in Washington
while we four stayed on two days
and soloed home parentless and glad
as the heroes of some children's book.
Please don't wave.

We found you home already, taken sick. Fever
burned in you, established as peat fire.
The eldest daughter, I was appointed minister
and anointed you with isopropyl, the glass-clear
cold of it splashing over all the unfamiliar
hot quiet of you, while Daddy phoned the hospital.
Please don't wave.

Now, mouse-soft, my daughter picks down the hall
to peek in at me and reassure herself
I'm where she left me: that I haven't
somehow vaporized, left her

through some dark fairy stealth,
my book still opened, the chair rocking, empty.
Please don't wave.

The doctors thought at first they
had it knocked: pneumonia. Penicillin
and you're cured. You did look better there
on Monday night. I can't even claim
I had a premonition when we left you in
that room, and from your high white bed
you waved.

Wire

These woods we ride
the horses in with such
complacency were
pasture fifty
years ago.

Unaccustomed now
to any greater
stature than this
in trees
we fail to recognize

how little
we should trust
their self-absorption.
Just beyond the trail
old fence wire waits
in random stretches,

barbed
as any childhood
...and
patient,
as if wire understood
the instinctive
suddenness of animals.

Spring Again

Spring again

that old chicanery
of sun-rinsed air
and nearly-finished flowers

The meadows
are tricked out
in sudden green,

the rivers gulping,
tearing to the sea

We are so eager to believe
the sleight-of-hand
the magic cotton-tailed trees

Smoke-white blossoms
cloud the air yet
beneath

our feet the earth
maintains her
old sure suck.

Bliss

April loves a challenge, choosing to split
the slab of winter-hardened earth with the
silk tongue of a crocus. She casts the stiffened
brooks as her fandango dancers. At first

they crack and groan, call her the cruelest of
taskmasters but April persists, persuades:
the streams ripple, sequined and agile. For
April even forgotten roadsides can

ruffle out in a froth of forsythia,
waving brash wands of membranous stars
that glitter like eternity, then float to
the ground, a wasted galaxy melting

into the land while this uterine
muscle of a month bears down, rousting
the fetuses each from their dark havens,
thrusting them naked and mewling into

the hungry light. The least of April's exploits
is lulling us: we are so eager to
ignore the hollow echo of the daffodils'
blare and the lithe red tulips' throats of snow.

Survivor

for my cousin, Donna

Jim's sister did the laundry right off.
She thought to spare me seeing
Gregory's things mixed with all the rest
as if nothing had changed: his
knee-stained jeans, underwear,
inside-out socks waiting to be washed,
like he'd be needing them for
next week's game. I know she meant
well but—that empty hamper—even
his dirty laundry had been taken from me.

We buried him in his favorite shirt
...an ordinary rugby shirt but I wanted
something he'd think would be comfortable;
the memory's still so fresh, standing there in Sears
picking out that shirt for "back-to-school"...
Little things are like that now: his last
school papers, the list he wrote for Santa,
his new birthday bike out in the garage,
not even dirty yet.

Muffin, his dog, used to drive me crazy;
dirt and commotion, dirt and commotion is
all I thought, but now Jim has her
"come" and "sit" and dance her little
jig, all the stuff Gregory taught her.

When he was born
it felt so clear to me:
this child is me, bone
of my bone, flesh of
my flesh. Then he's growing
up—they grow up so quickly—and
you kind of talk yourself
out of being so attached.
But Gregory, with you

lying there, all those
careful lines we drew
erase, and I can't seem
to understand, what is it
that survives of me
if not you?

The Suicide's Mother

I'd have thought the horses
would spook to see you
dangling so; snorted, whinnied,
knocked hooves against their doors,
but I didn't hear a thing.

The horses waited there
expectantly in the morning light
as if it seemed to them you could
descend at any moment and parcel out
their breakfast grain like any
ordinary day. Your high stillness
failed to frighten them
the way it frightens me.

Others spooked them later: the yard
over-filled with cars, police cruisers,
the ambulance. Esperanza, your favorite,
thrashed in her stall like a trapped bird
when the man edged out along the rafter
to release you, redeem
what could be redeemed
of your cold silence.

One policeman asked me
if I could answer why.
He asked it and his notebook
was opened to fresh paper but
he looked far off beyond my shoulder
as he spoke.

This day is ending now.
The stableyard is cleared at last;
the horses fed and bedded for the night
by other hands than yours.
In the garden I am gathering

the narrowed orange throats
of spent day lilies, while
from the evening grasses, moths,
very small, white moths,
ascend.

The Attraction of Hurricanes

A storm so utterly storm
you could smell it coming.
I loved the way it altered
everything, the majesty
of a force that brought
all the daddies home from work
and made the maple trees
bow down like grass; mighty presence
to tear away electric lines and center
the family by the fireplace popping corn
and playing Monopoly. We watched
the melee through the windows, from
a distance for fear of flying debris:
the storm sucked color out as efficiently
as dusk or dawn, our familiar yard in shades
of gray and blurred with blown rain, as
indistinct as a transmission on our
recently acquired TV sets.

After one of the storms—Carol, Donna?—
when the eye had passed, my father
took us down to the ocean's edge at
Newport just to see what might be left.
It needed all his knowledge of back roads
to find intact pavement to the shore
but he got us there to view the concrete
sea wall heaved up on the lawn across
the road, and the long curve of road itself
lost to the boiling stew of surf.

That ocean inspired a peculiar joy,
love even, swelled as it was with power,
roiled and reveling not in its power over
anything, but in its power purely,
wholly removed from insight or intent,
completely and appallingly simple.

Bonding

Whatever my value other
times, now I am
beside the point.
Out there in October's
orange light my son, 11 years,
strains to control the
tractor hydraulics: tipping,
lifting, holding, dropping the
implacable metal arms in
labored counterpoint to his father's
shouts: *other way, little more, little
more, hold it* while beneath
the brute indifferent bulk
his father struggles to seat
the recalcitrant bucket loader:
junctures groan and balk,
voices rise and fall
amidst the palpable pulsations
of engine roar, until, somehow
fittings finally align closely enough
and across the autumn air
I hear at last that bell-bright ring
of coupling pins
hammered home.

Mirrored

The weight of living
years together
flattens out emotion;
just now I don't want
to fit so freely to you:
your back's known curve,
the easy tangle of our legs together,
even the crease of
your eyes as you smile,
hollow me:
already doors are closing,
the hallway dims.

Do you mind waking
with me still here?
You know it isn't
you that I resent
but rather, knowing

loss is mirror silver
on our gains,
achievements
glitter back our limitations.

Remorseless Loyalty

Orange

Winter sun
spills in a heat-magnified pool
through the southern window.

I sit
soaking in the spillway
peeling an orange as if
husking the sun.

Washed with light, the fragrant fruit
opening, opening
to membrane
in my hands, I
consume peacefully,
absorbent
as God.

Thanksgiving

In the black and snow-patched
night, we're pulled from sleep

by the chill chuckle of coyotes
sweeping the hillside. We spoon

into one another's warmth
and consider

the keen exuberance
of those unseen shapes,

thrilling to their work.
In the morning's aftermath,

we tangle, tender, hearts
pulsing against one another,

breath a small wind in one
another's ear, flicker of fingers

to soothe away for now
the night, its livid song.

He-Goat

Does the ram caught
by the horn in the thicket
ache to be free
of protuberance, finished
with thrust   and bury?

Pinned there in the
punishment of sun, does he
dream smooth lines and liquidity,
dream blue?

In time he hears
human voices:
do those distract him with hope
or fear?

Abram's eye
and blade
turn to him at last
in a glare
of transformation.

Samhain
poem found in Ireland, October 1990

On this night the door between
the living and the dead cracks
and spirits freely roam. Samhain
the Druids called it, summer's end,
and they kindled then the new fire,
the fire of peace, and burnt horses
in sacrifices of praise and protection.
Hallowe'en we call it now, and the fires
burn more fantastically than ever; in
old Ireland the devil holds that door
wedged open with his foot.

Jack-o'-lanterns blaze against November's
edge now; hollowed out, incendiary vegetables,
they flick their orange, pentacostal tongues
in the lingua franca of foreboding. A
peculiarly Irish enigma: who but the Irish
light their own route to damnation with a grin?

In Derry, in Newry this year
the I.R.A. created jack-o'-lanterns
in explosive-laden vans. They strapped
civilian drivers forcibly in
the seats while gunmen held the
driver's families hostage and
marksmen shadowed the chosen
priests on the grim processional
to British army checkpoints. What hungers
can such sacrifices satiate?

Will the Sidhe never cease
to shriek across this land?
Burned down to the sharp mean nub,
Ireland feeds the flames
with her own selves and the fire
never dampens.

Cast

The creature we call the horse was never
meant to be stabled, and can
stumble against his evident
unsuitability at any point;
just the small indulgence
of a roll in the shavings can
leave him wedged upended against
the wall, all grace overturned, the
legs stampeding helplessly in air.

It's called cast,
and in the alarm of flightlessness,
horses can struggle with force enough
to flop their innards: a twist
only surgery or death
can then release.

You who latched the door
are responsible. Sleep lightly.
When you hear the scrambling
in the night, you must
go to him in your bedclothes,
reach in among the maelstrom
of hooves, grasp firmly the far
pastern, and pull
the panic into yourself.

Particles

The struck dog's eyes glazed
in a look of surprise
the look of one
who didn't mean to be dead,
didn't mean to cause
this trouble.

Back in the house
after burial,
tufts of dog hair
under tables,
clinging to upholstery,
yesterday's annoyance
now golden, innocent
in the altered light.

Moment after particular
moment slips past:
mutable to immutable
so effortlessly.

Effortless,
and so beyond
our efforts.

List for a Blue Day

I look to the ease of ordinary things, the grace of dailiness:

the fresh pleasure of lined paper and a new pen;

the sure glide of the car uncurling from a tight parking space;

the radiant hum and heat of the young in classrooms, hallways,
   seeking, ripe;

the juice of poetry;

the bright geometry of towels stacked in the closet, or spoons
   nested in the drawer, content;

the effervescent arrhythmia of the store clerk's song while he
   believes himself alone;

shoes quietly in closets, under beds, shaped by what they've
   known, and may know again;

the sleek containment of locust seeds, unblinking black eyes in
   their silvered pods;

the image Milt invokes for us of Jerusalem's Western Wall,
   tongues of language in the crevices, stones flickering into
   prayer;

the smudge of earth's shadow stroking the moon's complete
   patience: slow rapture, as if, at that remove, our touch
   were infinitely tender;

the lane markers, like geese in chevrons as I skim home in the
   center lane, coasting the updrafts;

the green float of speedometer numerals in the dark before me:
   miles melt at that temperature, and I am sailing into our vil-
   lage;

the nubble of flannel, warmed sheets, electric, and the fit, ah,
the fit of our bodies together.

I will always know this.

Iridescent

What is it that feels
like connection?

Driving by, isolated
in my car, I see you
on the bike, open to air and rain
and, it would appear, happiness:
your dark face a steady
pleasure, the asphalt of the
road just slicking up with
the rain, your marine green
trousers pumping pumping
the bike, which
trembles as you steer
one-handed, your other hand
is triumphant with
the shining green plentitude
of fish on your string.

And I imagine you offer willingly,
if only for that moment,
the iridescent gift
of beholding you
exactly as you are.

Repair

Walking today where I walked yesterday, the
day before, the   days before, I am happy
now in the   snowfall's clean
erasure.   In the lee of
the   hill's crest
I   come upon
a   casting
in   the
snow   like the
figures   children
trace—flat   out, their
arms flailing   into wings—
except the mold   left here a horse
has scooped out in   non-metaphoric content.
Her absented imprint makes a well for winter
sunlight: voiceless, and oracular as stone.

Lady Writing a Letter

Vermeer's vocabulary
is light and shadow. Stucco
and shutter resolutely define
the canvas's space, collecting

shade in a dark pool the table top,
and the woman's torso only just
emerge from. On the table is the letter
she is writing, the quill

stilled now in her hand.
Beside her hand, a strand
of pearls, the harvested
fruit of the folded oyster.

The lady wears yellow
silk, the orpiment
gold pulses against
the dusk of that room.

Trimming her jacket, dark-flecked
white squirrel rings her wrists
and neck, a plush reminder
of what survives.

Rising from the fur her face turns
to offer us her broad openness,
that radiant and vulnerable center
of all that waits in gloom around her.

How the Painter Hungers
Vermeer's Lady Writing a Letter

My mother-in-law, Maria, is a discreet
and practical woman: in the interests
of art and income, she grants me
a necessary latitude we contrive
to shield from her daughter. Maria understands,
as Catherina never would, how the painter hungers
for the shape his brush pursues: the porcelain
curve of a bowl, the pearlescent
folds of the oyster on its shell, or
a woman draped in fur and silk,
the wanton necklace dropped by her hand.

Maria indulges me, but indulgence
has its limits. There are always limits.
And so, much as one misdirects the eye
until flat appears flesh, substantial
and warm, one distracts one's own heart
with luster, sheen. I am an acolyte now
to the plushness of light, consecrated
to the sacrament of shadows.
I subsist on the rituals of shape,
proportion, dimension.
Pure hue is my sustaining eucharist,
and I crave radiance like air.

The Widow's Arms

The widow's arms are a new-mown lawn,
fragrant with loss, and memory.

Her spoon ticks its singular note:
day spins in its vortex.

The face of the widow
is an avalanche-slicked ravine, and the poles probing.

Her spring opens everywhere
the suck of its mud mouths.

The widow's eyes
are juncos watched by the hawk;

Her oven door shuts tight
against the darkness harbored there;

For the widow, summer simmers with flowers,
rose red, and the glare of gladioli;

Her heart is an engine,
a muscle thoughtless and strong;

The widow's stairs rise into recurrence,
a stubborn melody whose lyrics cannot be recalled.

The widow's chair is deep as snow.
The widow's shoes walk everywhere alone.

Her autumn is an old coat,
spent ticket stub in with the pocket lint;

The widow's hours are children
who can never be fed enough;

Her winter is runic and carved;
The widow's bed is a train

rocking out into the trackless prairie,
beneath the dark indifference of the stars.

Tag

Acrochordon is the medical term:
fleshy little pendants, impish tongues
of tissue sticking out
from your neck, underarms, the
crepe-fine skin of the eyelids,
or groin, developing after
midlife, puckish markers
of just where you're at.

The common name is
skin tag, and I think,
tag,

you're it, my sneakered
feet, the fisted heart in my chest
pounding, the grass, the blurring
trees pulsing as I run, twirl, swirl, whirl, only just
evading, and the murmurous applauding
of the many-handed maple we race beneath,
the laughter in the gathering
twilight, and still the patient
streetlights poised to flicker on,
calling us out of this world,
this rush, this beat, calling us
home.

Forecast

Mothers are like weather:

my sunshine days long past
the children shovel me off their paths
and at last submit to umbrellas,
handy now to
deflect me.

The children are eager
to whip up
their own meteorology.

Mothers silver
into moons, turning their faces
towards, and away,
towards, and away, their wordless
yearning tugging
deep within the oceans.

Fresh

Wind blows through the emptiness
of any warnings I may have received:
I am as unprepared as I have to be.

The children inhale happily that fresh
breeze and lug the cartons
of their ambitions up the stairs,
bantering as they unpack
and move into the life
I haven't finished with yet.
They shuffle the furniture and fashion
shelves from the boards and cinder blocks
of unfinished desires, consulting
anyone but me.

Awake in the breathing dark,
her lover asleep beside her,
passing cars glimmer
incandescent figures
on the walls and ceilings.
Does my daughter feel as porous as I did
with the life that will be hers
flickering softly about her,
soaking in?

Stand By

The wood stove is feeling peppy.
Past midnight, and I'm weary but
the logs I fed the fire twenty minutes
ago are chortling, gulping at the air they're
sucking in at every seam. I've
shut the vent, closed down the damper, still
they're roaring merrily up the stovepipe
sizzling, shifting, popping sap
like gum between the teeth, beaming
their megawatts in all directions, hell-bent
on lighting up the party, consuming
themselves in a sudden splurge
of all they've ever waited for and I

am hovering there as anxious
and disregarded as any parent
standing by.

Comparing Scars
for my son, on his leaving home

You took the exit that left my abdomen
smiling wryly as the Mona Lisa, but I know
what she's thinking. Life leaves its mark.

At twelve, that accident left
your leg cored out to bone, the surgeon
plucking gravel from the periosteum

while I held your eyes in mine and you
wrung and bundled the phalanges
of my hand like talismanic sticks

I never thought to ask, as the intern finally asked,
Couldn't he have morphine? To each life
its agonies.

At the age you are now, I was motherless
buoyant with the luck of my abandonment,
fingering the scars of my own choices

Your scars are all your
own now. I take comfort where I can:
the rain, and how the lawn's emptied

expanse erupts in parasols
of fungus, the earth's unforgotten
memory of forest.

Vows

We stood in a garden and promised
to do the best we could.
It was the 70's:
flowers in my hair, you in a billowy shirt.

Then, I had looked for the words
to express exactly how far I believed
promises could stretch, knowing

the future is always dangerously animate,
like the edges of old maps, emblazoned
with monsters and the words:
Here be dragons.

Our dragon now is the forked tongue
of the trigeminal nerve flickering
through the left side of your face
like the burn of a lightening strike
repeating and repeating, a condition
for which they have treatments
but no cure.

Both of us miss
who you used to be.

We surge over the edge of the map
in the same flotilla
but on separate ships

that long expanse of ocean
we have crossed to reach here
swallowed in fog.

Out here mortality thumps
leviathan against our hulls:

leaving you isn't what I think about.

What I feel, as you must as well
is hammered, gold
to airy thinness beat:

two battered foils
bruised, but shimmering
with the strength we have.

Losing Greta

1.

Returning starlings clamor: a fist of birds
clenching and unclenching in the air.
The scribbled landscape
of mud and melting snow is a sketch
of losses we have yet to name.

2.

Friends say: *we'll keep you
in our prayers.*
Who could fail to cherish
sheltering in that glade?

3.

In the end, the undertow
must be alluring.
Too far now
from shore to see us waving,
has the cold current
at last begun
to feel like home?

4.

What tips the balance
is imperceptible:
after weeks
seeming to hover
at this brink,
the daffodils bloom.

Persephone Converses with the Snow

Slipping free of the fissure, Persephone tells the snow,
you've got the touch. She stretches out and sweeps
snow angels with her arms and legs; her goddess
robe balls up along her thighs and Persephone
laughs, her laugh the sound of freshets
breaking free from ice.

Persephone admires the snow for its alabaster coolness.
I know a thing or two about purity, she notes, smoothing
down her hair, her robe. Shaking the underworld from her soles,
Persephone tells the snow how luscious
are the snow's cold shoulders.

Persephone rolls and pats the snow into featureless, ovoid
figures she leaves behind without a backward glance.
Rays of winter-flattened grass pant out like tongues
where she has rolled the snow up. Persephone assures
the snow she understands its yielding—its yielding,
and its icy carapace glittering like skulls in moonlight.

Watching the wine stains of earth opening now beneath
the trees, Persephone appeals to the snow's patience.
Persephone has known patience. Has wound
the roots below the earth in skeins, and woven
scarves of waiting on the loom of her own finger bones.

Persephone tells the snow, don't go. I am tired of sacrifice.

The snow tells Persephone, you're too hot to handle.
I sizzle at your touch. My wings are weeping
where you've stroked me, but I'll fly all the while.
The snow believes in its crystal heart it has new things
to say, but then the snow blanks out, a blur of frozen verbs.
Now the snow's speech is peppered with sand, spray-painted
with urine, punctuated with scat. Mud and I, we're the original
poly-vocal texts, the snow proclaims.

Settling in, the snow tells Persephone a winter's tale.
She's heard it all before. She's well aware what order costs,
and just who pays the price. The snow murmurs,
I repeat whatever I hear with absolute fidelity.
My loyalty is a kind of forgetting. In the forgetting,
all becomes pure. I am the memory of landscape.

Now the snow shimmers, a sleek sheen
beneath the mallow radiance of stars.
The snow tells Persephone its silence.

Persephone's are just the ears for silence.

Gelding the Two-Year-Old

The colt sways and struggles for balance
while we let the local anesthesia work;
by then the tranquilizer is wearing thin
so we twitch him and work quickly;
the vet slits the pouch
and clamps off the smooth fibrous ball;
we wait,
for the pressure to cauterize I guess;
the testicle is already
separate, unclamp
and it comes away;
the vet tosses the small
mass to a corner of the stall.
Now the other side.
The colt thrusts and kicks his hind legs,
the tail switches uncomfortably;
the wound steams in the chill air.

Pulse

It's the pulse of concealed wings
that pulls me:
  that beating
    in the heart
of the bush you pass
at twilight.

There is
  nothing symbolic
about this boy,
    he is
      wholly
        substantial
      immediate
          one might say real

Even his pale
  scarred wrists,
burned the Halloween he was seven
when the bigger boys smashed
about in the smaller boys' game of Gaelic
and it happened to be him
who fell into the Druid fire, happened
to be him, as it
can happen to be anyone,
          even those
            wrists are not
                symbolic.

The first thing,
in fact the only thing,
the boy notices here that prompts the words:
    "like in Ireland" is
    a Life magazine photo
of land mine victims in what had been
Yugoslavia. The light
    in the Bosnian clinic is

unobstructed,
             undiluted as
photos shot in black and white "Did you
             see the wee one
   on the end with no legs?" he asks.
      This happening to be
             is unaccountable
      and unquenchable, there
          is nothing
             totemic
             about
      this boy.

He sleeps peacefully here
in the morning birdsong despite
being better accustomed to
traffic sounds and the chatter
of Brits on duty at the checkpoint
the soldiers have chosen to build
by his house. His family thought
it unnerving to step out
of the house, pocketbook, school bag,
or tool kit in hand, and find
the young Brits lounging
on the step, weapons casually
slung, so the family
        got a dog
   to alert them when
      someone was about. Not,
          you understand,
      a symbolic dog, but
   a tan and white
   Jack Russell terrier named Rusty
eager as any dog
to be part of boyish errands
and adventures and so
effective an alarm
that the soldiers
grew annoyed and stole him.

Can you talk to the police here?
he asks me, a wholly
   concrete and specific question
      at home you can speak
      if spoken to but never
start a conversation or the IRA
might suspect you: critical
advice boys far younger
than twelve have by heart

so no one considers asking
what became of the dog but
two years pass and Rusty's on the step,
come home, not an emblem
but a warm package of dog
that sleeps on your bed (as perhaps
      he slept for two years on
         some unknown homesick soldier's bed)
and roams the field with you
once again. Life is
as life is

               for even this boy's open

               smile, his

               joy at the buoyancy to a

               soccer ball: toe-tap, toe-tap, and fly

         his open

               enthusiasm plunging

         into into the Atlantic surf—these things

               are not symbolic but

                  momentary

momentously

    vital

  vulnerable

    and beating

      at the heart.

for Tommy

Slieve League
County Donegal, Ireland

Cliffs draw us, as margins must: that limitless curiosity limits excite.
It's exactly the 600 meters of granite verticality that insinuates

closer, let me show you. Our thirst for clarity runs that deep.
The glittering little lake at Bunglass Point observes unblinking

as tourists and family groups head off along the ridge; there
at Amharc Mor, "the good view," a sketchy fence suggests

but well beyond, the man and boy stroll, and a girl sits leaned
against a stone, turning the pages to her book, rehearsing nonchalance.

This high up, the breathing of the sea is barely audible.
Watchers cross and re-cross the glass distance to the waves,

imagining the release, almost welcome in the manageable
summer air. Daydreams. Less than vapor. Assume instead

the composure of the heather. After the cliff walkers
return to their domestic suppers, after the noisome

cars reload and wend back, sunset stains the stones
mortal red and shadowed ambergris. In the mobile dark

of borderland the sea repeats without complaint
the siren song of its remorseless loyalty.

Describing Derroe
County Galway

The word needed has no mastery in it.

Groomed by hand with scythe and rake
the fields grow sleek with grass:
a villanelle of blades
that lick the walls and whisper to the air
syllables of their own ancient litany.

Do not misread the grace note
of human effort: the hives
of harvested hay are a providence, yet
nothing is owed,
nothing earned:

under the bright palm of the sky
moment by moment murmurs into memory
or silence:

that enduring
urge of continuance
wheels on.

The Green Road

Over Killary Harbor the sharp-sloped hills
rise steeply out of the drowned valley,
a grass-softened chalice of stone
that even on this sunny day collects
and cups mist rising from the water's surface:

a yielding presence we ride through
on rented horses, stolid Irish draughts
who carry us slack-reined
along "the green road," a public
works project the British dreamed up
in the famine year of 1848.

Immaculate capitalists, the Brits
were loath to dole out money
the starving hadn't earned and so
their humanitarian relief put
malnourished men to body-breaking work

constructing roads that led only
to the green of nature, or webs
of stone walls whose sole purpose
was the pay check that could not
buy food enough to restore even
the energy it cost to earn it,

let alone to feed the wasted,
waiting children, mouths stained green
with grass, the verdant grass of Ireland,
flourishing outside the property lines
like an offering, unclaimed, lush
and incapable of sustaining them.

When men died out on the works,
there could be no thought
of carrying them home. Their fellows

spared precious effort just to bury them
where they fell, unshrouded, unmarked
beside the futile road or wall.

Long years later, the grass abides
and these roads remain unforgotten
elegies carrying us deep
into the past's persistence,
a hymn we ride
into the silver rain.

Shimmer

Faith
in those narratives of larger meaning
is a fat salmon of knowledge

but the compact
completeness of those silver stories
can seem a glut of sweet flesh

and fading
scales to those of us for whom
meaning is a small glitter through the current,

shimmering,
quick
and not to be counted upon.

Rite

for Gregory at thirteen

When I hear the hunter's
shots tell their quick
tale in the heart
of our November woods
I know at once the vulnerability
everything my son knew
until now has in the face
of the trembling
silence to follow.

In the stripped woods
he kneels with the hunter
beside the musky stillness.

The gap the knife opens
envelops him easily.

Glistening in its silver sac
what they mean to leave
behind they leave there
to cool in the darkening wood.

What my son knows now
they truss
and drag
deliberately home.

Print

A silver muscle of ice
shuts up the brook.
In the canopy, hardwoods

crack their knuckles and sway,
inward as adolescents.
The slender birches lurch

and rattle their stiffened fingers
while a deer swivels
the antennae of her ears,

scooping the air for warning
sounds, and prints the snow
with the sharp hearts of her hooves.

Spring at 41

I walked the woods early today.
Sunlight advanced before me
across the hill's crest as if
the light and warmth were mesh,
a solar seine delicately, deliberately opening
out in the morning's first cast. Birdsong
and frog trill were a pulse,
a felt sound in that spring air.
Bluets, violets, strawblossoms, and
spring beauties crowded my path in such
profusion I could imagine
they welcomed me much
as I welcomed them. My own arms
swung at my sides, in the line
of sight, my skin crimped yet
with the imprint of the bedsheets,
wrinkled like a baby's cheek from the crib.
This was a kind of grace to behold and
for the moment I felt
renewable as the morning.

Island

News like that is a cave,
or an island you've washed up on
far from the life you used to have.

Frightening as they are, you watch,
absorbed, the brain making
thoughts, that sensation
of making suddenly tactile
and cherished as a penitent's rosary beads

but you are not praying,
only alert to the moment,

attentive as any castaway
swept up on an alien shore.

Brainstorm

In the aftermath the neurosurgeon
orders up an angiogram.
The one-eyed catheter snakes in,
supple cyclops burrowing through.

To look, to look away?
There is no sense
in which you are not interested.

Dye enters one branch
at a time, a smoldering blush
you feel deep in the brain
while the images bloom
on the screen: chokecherry, hawthorn,

the many-fingered tributaries
of a fertile delta,
petalled flame,

all the lovely, membranous
underbrush that succors
the brain

revealed like an insight,
like the blue-white
muscle of lightening

that ruptures the night
in the irreplaceable instant.

My Love Is Like A...

You need to understand how shopworn
all the furniture of love poems has become,
how the springs have sprung from the sofas

of human yearning, the nub worn off
the upholstery of embraces, even
the floor lamps of long glances winking out.

Did any of those decorating projects
of the past really succeed? All those
roses, rhymes, full moons and shepherds...

I have no *House Beautiful* of poems to offer you,
but come, I've taken the washed sheets in
sweet from the sun...

we'll make up our bed together now.

Carpe Diem

The urgent season is upon us.
Innumerable cotyledons thrust
green elbows up through chill, dark humus;

peepers and green frogs trill their outsize lust
songs from each least amnion of moisture.
Those transparent-skinned pools combust

in a clouded roil at just the pressure
of a shadow. It's that vulnerability
of being alive, exposed to the vigour

of others' hungers, and impelled by your own rapacity.
Birds bicker and breed behind the screen
of infant leaves, while the cat intently, particularly,

adjusts the lay of every hair and licks clean
her paws. Cock's tail fronds spread from the peony stems
the stems knobbed with hard-fisted buds, their bronze-green

sepals sticky with sweet exudate. Ants come, swarm
the stalks, and bite the stuck fists into bloom.

The Richard Snyder Publication Series

This book is the eighth book in a series honoring the memory of Richard Snyder (1925-1986), poet, fiction writer, playwright and longtime professor of English at Ashland University. Snyder served for fifteen years as English Department chair, and was co-founder (in 1969) and co-editor of the Ashland Poetry Press, an adjunct of the university. He was also co-founder of the Creative Writing major at the school, one of the first on the undergraduate level in the country. In selecting the manuscript for this book, the editors kept in mind Snyder's tenacious dedication to craftsmanship and thematic integrity.

Snyder Award Winners:
1997: Wendy Battin for *Little Apocalypse*
1998: David Ray for *Demons in the Diner*
1999: Philip Brady for *Weal*
2000: Jan Lee Ande for *Instructions for Walking on Water*
2001: Corrinne Clegg Hales for *Separate Escapes*
2002: Carol Barrett for *Calling in the Bones*
2003: Vern Rutsala for *The Moment's Equation*
2004: Christine Gelineau for *Remorseless Loyalty*